ABC

ALPHABET RHYMES

Please visit our web site at: www.garethstevens.com
For a free color catalog describing Gareth Stevens Publishing's
list of high-quality books and multimedia programs, call
1-800-542-2595 (USA) or 1-800-387-3178 (Canada).
Gareth Stevens Publishing's fax: (414) 332-3567.

Library of Congress Cataloging-in-Publication Data available upon request from publisher.
Fax (414) 336-0157 for the attention of the Publishing Records Department.

ISBN 0-8368-4095-X

First published in 2004 by
Gareth Stevens Publishing
A World Almanac Education Group Company
330 West Olive Street, Suite 100
Milwaukee, Wisconsin 53212 USA

Copyright © 2004 by Nancy Hall, Inc.

Gareth Stevens series editor: Dorothy L. Gibbs
Gareth Stevens graphic designer: Kami M. Koenig

Printed in the United States of America

1 2 3 4 5 6 7 8 9 08 07 06 05 04

ABC

ALPHABET RHYMES

by Matt Mitter • illustrations by Doug Cushman

Gareth Stevens Publishing
A WORLD ALMANAC EDUCATION GROUP COMPANY

Each night, the little wildcat
    begs his mom, "Read to me, please!"
He loves to hear his favorite book
    of noisy ABCs!

A is for an angry **APE**
    who hollers all night long.

B is for a bunch of **BELLS**
    that bing and bang and bong.

5

C is for a copper **CANNON**, firing cannonballs.

D is for a dungeon **DOOR** that slams and shakes the walls.

E is for two **ELEPHANTS**, stampeding through the halls.

6

F is for a **FIRE TRUCK**
that's off to fight a fire.

G is for the **GHOSTS** that groan
together in a choir.

H is for a **HIPPO**
that is learning how to dive.

I is for the **INSECTS**
that are swarming
'round the hive.

J is for a **JACKHAMMER**
that's digging up the drive.

K is for a kid's **KAZOO** — a noise you can't ignore.

L is for the lazy **LION**,
practicing its roar.

M is for a mob of **MICE** that munch on many cheeses.

N is for a noisy **NOSE**

that sniffles, snorts, and sneezes.

O is for an **ORGAN**,
on which
only ogres
pound.

P is for **PROPELLERS**,
spinning loudly 'round and 'round.

Q . . . well, Q's for **QUIET**,
and it means "don't make a sound."

R is for a **ROLLER COASTER**, racing 'round a loop.

S is for a **SKELETON** that stumbled on the stoop.

12

T is for a **TUBA** and a trumpet and trombone.

U is for a **UKULELE**
you can play alone.

V is for a **VACUUM CLEANER**, vrooming 'cross the floor.

W is for the **WOLVES** that howl outside the door.

A silent X will mark the spot
where buried treasure lies.

Y is for a sleepy **YAWN**.
Good night.
Now, close your eyes.

"Sweet dreams," the
wildcat's mother said,
then kissed him tenderly.
"But, Mom," he mumbled,
"we're not done.

We didn't get to Z ZZZZZzzzzz . . ."

15

To Parents and Teachers:

Helping children learn the alphabet is fun. You can play alphabet games almost anywhere! Point to a passing truck and ask, "Does the word 'truck' start with a C or a T?" You can point to almost any object outdoors, around the house, or in picture books. You might want to start with the pictures below.

Does start with a **V** or a **C**?

Does start with an **L** or a **D**?

Does start with an **M** or a **W**?